# HELPERS
## AT MY CHURCH

*Mary Sue White*

*Pictures by Beatrice Derwinski*

Library of Congress Catalog Card Number 59-5868

**Second Printing**

©1959

BROADMAN PRESS • Nashville, Tennessee

# THE PASTOR IS A HELPER
# AT MY CHURCH

My pastor helps me
  to know about God.
He reads to us from the Bible
  about God and his love.
He asks us all to pray.

I try to be as still as I can
and listen to what
my pastor says.
When I pray, I bow my head
and shut my eyes.
Then I talk to God.

The pastor visits our room.
He helps us to understand
that God is
our Heavenly Father.
He tells us how
we can help God.

Sometimes we go with my pastor
to his office.
We listen while he tells us
about his work.
We talk to God
while we are there.

My pastor helps people all week.
He visits in homes
    to ask people to come
    to our church.
He visits in homes
    to tell people about Jesus.

He goes to see people
who are sick.
One time he visited me
when I was in the hospital.
I was glad he came.

MANY PEOPLE HELP
THE PASTOR WITH
THE CHURCH SERVICES.

The organist plays for my church.
The pianist plays too.
Sometimes the music is soft
and slow.
Sometimes it sounds like flutes.
Other times it sounds
like ringing bells.

The music in my church
   makes me feel good all over.
It helps me to be quiet and still,
   and feel that God is near.

The choir sings together.
The music sounds clear and sweet.
The choir helps us
    to sing our praise
    and thanks to God.

I like to sing too.
I watch the music director
and sing with the choir.

The music director in my church
helps me learn to sing
with others.
He tells us what to do
when he moves
his hands around.

I know this song.
You can sing it too.

# I'M A HELPER

I'm a help - er  in  my church.

There are man - y  things to  do.

I  can bow my  head and pray;
I  can lis - ten  qui - et - ly,
I  can share my  toys  at  play;
I  can sing so  joy - ful - ly;

I  can talk to  God  this  way.
When  my teach - er  reads  to  me.
Help my friends be  kind and gay.
Friends will want to  sing with  me.

The ushers help us when we go
    to the church service.
Some of them meet us at the door.
They speak to us
    and shake our hands.
They give us a bulletin.
Later on they take the offering.

I like to give my offering.
When I give my money
    I help to buy things
    for my church.
I help to tell other people
    about Jesus.

My teacher is a helper
in my church.
She helps us learn
about God and Jesus.
She tells us stories from the Bible.
Sometimes she shows us pictures
about the stories she tells.
Other times we play out
the story she tells.

My teacher helps me to tell others
about Jesus.
We went to visit a man
who could not come to church.
We gave him something
we had made.
We wanted him to know
that God loves him.

Miss Ann helps in my room.
She keeps the names
    of children who come
    to church.
She finds out about those
    who do not come each time.

One day Bill was not at church.
I made a card and sent to him.
The card said,

Dear Bill,
I miss you.
Hurry back to church!

It was good to have Bill
back with us.

My Grandmother is a helper
in my church.
She goes to see each new baby.
She gives the baby's mother
something to read.
She asks the mother
to bring the baby to church.

My friends and I wanted to help
    Grandmother with her work.
We made a pocket folder
    to carry her papers.
Now the papers do not fall
    on the floor while she talks
    with the mothers.

The church librarian helps me
to find the books I like.
She asks me to write my name
on a card so she will know
who has the book.
She tells me when to bring
the book back.

I try to be quiet in the library
and look at a lot of books.
Sometimes I stay to help
the librarian.
She lets me stack the books
on her table.
I help her put the chairs back
in their places.

Mr. Hill helps to get our church
ready for worship.
He opens the doors
and turns on the lights.
He keeps the church clean
for our people.

One spring we planted bulbs.
We gave them water
   and put them in the sun.
When they were ready to bloom,
   we gave them to Mr. Hill.
We wanted to thank him
   for being a good church helper.

Our church sends missionaries
   to tell others about Jesus.
One time one of the missionaries
   came to visit our church.
She told us how we could help
   boys and girls
   who do not know Jesus.

We help the missionaries
to tell others about Jesus.
We send books.
We send toys.
We send church papers.
It is fun to send gifts
to friends we do not know.

1134

ARE THERE SOME
OTHER PEOPLE
WHO HELP
IN YOUR CHURCH?


DO YOU KNOW
WHO THEY ARE?


DO YOU KNOW
WHAT THEY DO?